COACHING LIKE A CHAMPION

COACHING LIKE A CHAMPION

EIGHT ESSENTIAL BUILDING BLOCKS FOR
TAKING ANY SPORTS PROGRAM TO THE NEXT LEVEL

STEVE MILLER

Library of Congress Control Number: 2018914896

ISBN:	Hardcover	978-1-9845-7290-5
	Softcover	978-1-9845-7289-9
	eBook	978-1-9845-7293-6

Print information available on the last page.

Rev. date: 01/10/2019

To order additional copies of this book, contact:
Xlibris
1-888-795-4274
www.Xlibris.com
Orders@Xlibris.com
789639

DEDICATION

To The Trimble High School Varsity football team that is a source of pride in their community as they constantly exemplify grit, energy and a commitment to always "hold the rope" for each other. This attitude has propelled one of the smallest schools in Ohio to repeated trips to the final four and become one of the dominant Division IV programs in the state. This is even more remarkable when you watch this team take the field. They are not big nor are they flashy. But they do not know the meaning of the word quit and those who have underestimated them have regretted it. They believe in "cause over self" and that individual achievement is accomplished through the giving of one's self to the goals and welfare of others.

A day after a tough loss in the state championship game, the players were in the weight room early preparing for the future and another playoff run. They understand the meaning of teamwork, commitment, sacrifice and endurance. They not only exude physical toughness but they are as mentally tough as any team I have ever seen. They know the importance of doing the hard thing over and over again, especially when they might not feel like doing it. They have experienced the benefits of doing so.

They represent a community where there may not be much material wealth but a whole lot of grit, determination, and a "pull yourself up by the bootstraps" mentality. This same community responded to a decision to demolish the beloved but collapsing football stadium. Many said replacing it with a new structure couldn't be done; too expensive for the incomes of most living in the township. The community refused to accept "can't" and proceeded to build a structure anyone would be proud to call their own.

I share all this because I want the team and community to know that in many ways they propelled me to write this book and see it to completion. The team and community have my respect and admiration.

CONTENTS

PREFACE

Many books have been written about being or becoming a champion with most relating to a *player's* qualities, characteristics and disposition. There is less written about *coaches'* attending to their work in building a champion's mindset. Why do we pay so much attention to the player's work ethic and characteristics and far less to how this is best carried out, not only for players but for other in our program as well? Should not coaches be just as eager to learn about the unique attributes and qualities necessary to transform their coaching approach by discovering within themselves how to assess existing strengths and the skills needed to cultivate if they are serious about responding to the challenges they face on a daily basis? Let me emphasize that this book is not meant to merely help you cope with daily pressures and stressors but to *masterfully* respond, *leverage* new opportunities, and *identify* the values and principles to propel you into the *Coaching like a Champion* class.

With this premise in mind I set out to determine from research as well as to reflect on my own experience what makes a coach excel and *Coach like a Champion*? I will describe in a practical way my findings so that current and aspiring coaches can apply them to their work. In addition, tips will be provided on working with others involved in your sports program and how to be attentive to their needs as they relate to building and elevating your program. These will be included in a **Hot Corner** and **Personal Game Plan Summary** at the conclusion of each chapter. * *Sorry for the baseball analogy but let me assure you this is not a baseball book. Findings can be applied to any sport as well as life.*

Part of the inspiration for this book comes from my friend and colleague Chris Stewart. Chris has had a successful career as a high school baseball coach and has authored the increasingly popular books, Building Champions: Coaching, Parenting, and Playing to Win in What Really Matters, and Coaching Life: Giving your best so others can be theirs! Chris posed an interesting question, "What is more important?" A. Coaching your sport or B. Coaching people. The answer to this question tells a lot about our coaching and particularly what motivates and drives us as coaches. Your answer is directly linked to why do you coach. Coach Stewart contends that many of us work hard at teaching the game with X's and O's but less attention to a player's mental strength, character development, the power of positive energy, promoting teamwork, and other skills that can be applied to life during and after one's mastery of hitting a ball, sinking a shot, kicking a field goal, or whatever.

So I want to thank Coach Stewart for prompting me to examine my coaching philosophy in light of what is important to me as a foundation – coaching the player versus coaching the game. We coach people, not a sport. That means we need to build relationships and develop trust. For me I have chosen to put more emphasis on my team, recognizing each member is an individual with gifts and talents that need nurturing. This includes the coach. The stronger each individual member is, the better we will be as a whole. So each of us can be all we can be, not only for ourselves but also for the good of the team. Coach Stewart reminded me that the *sport* can be used to achieve something special in the players and that great coaches should continually be working on themselves and their interpersonal skills. Thanks Chris for helping me put this in perspective and refocusing my coaching approach to building champions as opposed to winning championships.

A coaching approach that demonstrates and reflects how the same characteristics we look for in players can become part of every coach's style will be presented in the chapters ahead in a practical, *Coaching like a Champion* framework, thus giving you the tools needed to succeed. Don't envy the champion – be the champion. I believe in intentionality and have worked in recent years to operationalize this concept. Intentionality means to live a life that is meaningful and fulfilling. It means you make thoughtful choices in your life. Being intentional means you actively interact and engage with others in your life. I say this because in order to adopt the *Coaching like Champion* mindset, it must be a conscious choice according to a set of beliefs internalized as a result of experience. It is my hope that you will become intentional about clarifying and applying your coaching beliefs as you work with players, coaches, parents and others stakeholders who look upon you as a transformational agent with enormous influence who can impact their lives in significant ways. Before there can be a "buy in from those in your program, there must first be a "believe in." The ball is in your hands. Will you run with it? Let's develop your game plan starting now.

ACKNOWLEDGEMENTS

Coaching like a Champion is a project brought to life thanks to the efforts of some special mentors, friends, and family. I am profoundly grateful to coaches, athletes, past and present, and school administrators who hired me to work in their systems and work with students.

Special thanks to:

All who have decided to pick this book up and make it part of your library – I appreciate it. It means a great deal to me.

My wife Peggy, who was patient as I sat at the computer many hours writing this book. She has always supported me and has rightfully earned the title of "team mom" over the years. She is my best friend, confidant, and willing to sit through double headers in brutal heat or cold. She has encouraged me no matter the endeavor. A friend once said, "If she likes baseball and is willing to discuss it, get her a ring and marry her". I did and no regrets.

My son Zach, who inspires me daily as he works with youth travel teams and demonstrates that coaching the person versus coaching the sport really does make a difference. It is all about compassionate discipline, structure, and learning outcomes with him and I am in awe at how he communicates this on a daily basis.

My daughter Amanda, who has taught me more about dealing with day-to-day human interactions than she could possibly know. She has a unique gift for communicating and connecting with her colleagues and I cherish our daily conversations.

William White, My first principal and athletic director who hired me to coach football and baseball.

Terry Dugan, who was the first head baseball coach I worked under and who taught me the value of organization, preparation, and patience.

Xilibris publishing company, for keeping me on task and moving the writing process along.

Chris Stewart, for the ongoing conversations about what it takes to become a champion. He also helped with book cover design and feedback/ review of the original manuscript.

Phil Faires, a former player, close friend, and current high school head coach who gives me the wonderful opportunity to work with him as a Varsity Assistant Baseball coach. He gives me great leeway in devising drills to develop our players and together we have had fun in helping them achieve success on and off the field. More often than not, I am the student learning from the cagy master. Players will run through a wall for Coach Faires. He will turn to me after observing a player's behavior and ask, "Can you imagine if a guy did that on our team when you were coaching us"? Then he proceeds to handle it in his own insightful way. It is no surprise he is a Hall of Fame coach. He cares deeply about all those involved in his program and they know it.

To my seven grandsons who keep me young by always asking, "Papa, want to play catch"?

INTRODUCTION

Today's coaches are hungry to know the unique qualities necessary to fulfill the expectations their institutions place on them. What happens when personal and institutional expectations collide or are unclear? *Coaching like a Champion* provides a distinctive approach to explain these and other dynamics of coaching.

The primary focus of this book will be on the specific skills, behaviors, characteristics and the performance indicators necessary to *Coach like a Champion*. Essential qualities for coaching with impact and excellence will be revealed.

Coaches will be able to assess their own coaching strengths and determine the skills they wish to cultivate. In developing new capabilities and applying versatile approaches to various situations, coaches can better respond to challenges, leverage new opportunities, and excel in their role. Complete with tools and resources for further developing coaching skills, this book enables coaches to:

- Reference action-steps for developing a *Coaching like a Champion* mindset
- Master and embody the inner characteristics, performance indicators, and values that the *Coaching like a Champion* mindset requires
- Take proactive steps toward reaching their goals
- Utilize core values and priorities to elevate themselves into a select group of coaches

Most coaches have some semblance of a strategic plan for their respective sport or sports. But to do something meaningful with it requires bold leadership as well as intense preparation. In a review of literature pertaining to success in sports, one characteristic surfacing across the board is having the *will* to prepare to win. This is not new news to those in coaching but I challenge you to ask yourself how you *apply* this concept to your coaching, especially the mental training aspects of working with athletes and coaches in your program. So much value is lost for all those concerned – players, administration, community, parents and fellow employees when coaches fail to prepare for the future and take an active role in shaping it. Are you a coach who thinks they are pretty good but so consumed with meeting the day-to-day demands of your job that you miss opportunities and overlook threats to your program? Have you ever asked yourself why didn't I think of that when reading about another coach's or program's success? Do you have good intentions but instead of thinking about possibilities and the future you are sucked into a conventional but reactionary problem-solving mode? Is it hard for you to break out of this vicious cycle and get ahead of the curve? The question is not whether you have routines but rather what routines you *should* have to keep your program viable and separate you from the competition.

So What Is It?

At this point, you are wondering what exactly is *Coaching like a Champion* all about? In my view this book is about providing solutions to common coaching problems and encompasses three main things:

- Fulfilling your regular coaching responsibilities in a proactive, forward-thinking way.
- Incorporating a specific collection of qualities and characteristics into your coaching style as you lead your team and execute your coaching objectives and plan.
- Provides added tools for dealing with the challenge of coaching and teaching others to live a life of excellence and fulfillment.

So what is the difference between normal, day-to-day coaching and a *Coaching like a Champion* mindset? The differences I've discovered center around the way the principles of a champion mindset are applied. Not only do champion coaches fulfill today's expectations, they also focus deeply about defining and focusing on a future agenda that hones in on the things that really matter. Defining a long term vision helps to allocate scarce resources wisely and channel the collective efforts of the team. This enables a coach to seize opportunities, head off threats, and achieve better results down the road. How would you like to find new ways to leverage new sources of competitive advantage and unique, value-added offerings for all those affected by your program?

Why does it Matter?

Coaching can be an extremely high pressure career and the average coach's tenure is shorter than many other professions. Challenges faced by first year coaches include:

- Balancing the demands of coaching and teaching
- Personal fatigue
- Securing community support
- Securing and caring for facilities and equipment
- Parental contact
- Keeping non-starting players motivated
- Motivating athletes to achieve consistent, peak performance

Coaches by and large do not see the challenges as too difficult for them to handle and feel reasonably prepared to deal with them. There are currently coaching education programs and conferences to prepare coaches for many of these challenges including:

- Mentoring programs providing emotional and tactical support for coaches
- Identifying proactive strategies to attract and retain qualified coaches.

- Encouraging first year coach's to coach no more than one sport during the first year to allow them to focus on their teaching responsibilities (* daunting, especially in smaller communities where attracting quality coaches is difficult)
- Future research to determine specific strategies experienced high school coaches use to avoid burnout

"The ultimate measure of a man is not where he stands in moments of comfort and convenience, but where he stands at times of challenges and controversy." (Martin Luther King) All the more reason for the premise of this book: Responses can be built to deal with these challenges and others that are sure to come if we choose to develop the mindset of *Coaching like a Champion.*

Would you like to elevate your performance and that of your assistants in order to maintain a competitive advantage? We have seen a shift in the requirements institutions have for their coaches in terms of competencies and behavior. But how do institutions support their coaches in light of challenges such as budget constraints, helicopter/lawnmower parents, changing player attitudes, gaining increased performance from athletes, engaging and exciting athletes in your program? How does a coach stay true to their coaching values and beliefs while at the same time change/adapt to meet the needs of their constituents, i.e., athletes and families? How can you adapt and change to remain relevant and effective in the future? How can you translate characteristics, values, and skills into *Coaching like a Champion?*

Successful coaching in the future will require creativity as a core coaching skill; right up there with **c**ommunication**, h**umility, **a**ccountability, **m**ental toughness**, p**assion, **i**ntegrity**, o**vercoming adversity, and a commitment to **n**ever settle for anything less than the best for your program while staying self-disciplined in the pursuit of excellence. There is no coincidence that that these leading letters combine to spell **champion**. Each characteristic will be given its own chapter in this book. I hope this acronym will aid in your understanding of a champion's mindset. And if this is not natural to you it can be learned. If you are a coach who is not looking for something "outside the box", then this book is not for you. If you are more interested in making your current box bigger to hold more of the same stuff in it or prefer short term, quick solutions and want some nice wrapping paper and pretty ribbon to make the old "box" look new, then this book is not for you.

It is rare to find anyone in sport who embraces a genuinely creative, innovative, "outside the box" approach to building a sustainably competitive high performance program: those who do are the real greats of high performance sport – the best of the best. You may be asking yourself, isn't it ok to just be good sometimes? My answer to that would be you should strive to become the best you can be at all times. I have been privileged to be part of many championships but there is always one that eludes you. Just being good isn't going to get your team to the final four or into that state championship game. You have to be at your best and believe you belong there.

Sport is inherently conservative and therefore it does not progress as fast as it could and the real breakthroughs in performance that are possible take far longer to evolve than they need to. Many times, in spite of the best solution often being obvious and readily available, we do not take it, preferring instead to adopt the solution which is most politically saleable or the solution which will cause the least possible "stakeholder" objections: we compromise creativity in the interest of political cohesion, cooperation and consensus.

Is this really ok? Is it so important to appease school administrators, athletic directors and even Boards of Education to compromise creativity skills thus killing coaching? In sports, where winning is about daring to be different, taking intelligent risks and introducing new breakthroughs by being unique, more innovative and creative than your competitors, compromising what's possible in the interest of what's politically tolerable is a recipe for disaster.

So What Can We Do?

Look inside ourselves. Everyone has the potential to be creative. We all dream. We all have imaginations. Creativity is taking the imagination and our dreams of what's possible and turning them into actions and coaching behaviors. Everyone has the potential to coach creatively but it means looking inside ourselves and listening to that little voice – you know the one - the "little voice that had lots of new ideas and crazy thoughts when we first started coaching – the same "little voice" we stopped listening to now that we are older, more experienced and started coaching like everyone else. Should we start listening to that "little voice" once again? Imagination leads to creativity and coaching is creativity. Why do we coach? To every "why" there is a "must". What must we do now in answer to this "why" question?

We have to look outside our sport. One can find anything, anytime, anywhere for free on the internet. So increase your odds of finding performance breakthroughs by looking outside your sport, to other coaches and athletes.

Look outside sport. Sport is but one small part of society. For example, the medical, business, educational and art professions are using multi-disciplinary teams to address problem solving and strategic planning. Do you think they might enhance your communication and learning environment you have created for your athletes? There are amazing things happening around the world in other fields of endeavor which have the potential to revolutionize your coaching program. All we have to do is look.

Coaching like a Champion cannot be practiced from a conservative perspective. The best ideas win and the best ideas come from the people who dare to be different, dare to dream, and who dare to think and do things that no one dreamed possible. Dream big. Imagine what's possible. Coach with creativity. Be your own champion. There are no limits.

Let's get started with the skills needed to *Coach like a Champion.*

CHAPTER 1

CHAMPION – COMMUNICATION

> "People cannot succeed in life without communicating effectively. It's not enough just to work hard. It's not enough to do a great job. To be successful, you need to learn how to really communicate with others."
>
> John Maxwell

Want to build a program with a champion's mindset? One of excellence? Start with your locker room first. Get it right with players. Then be sure you have coaches and others in your program on the same page. Inside/Out Coaching author Joe Ehrman discusses how coaches have a tremendous platform to impact young people in ways that no one else can except perhaps the parents. Communicating is really connecting with people and relating to them in a way that increases our influence with them. By doing so, we help them and us as coaches reach our true potential. The question is not *are* we communicating but *how* and *what* are we communicating. And most importantly, are we connecting?

Communication is collaborative; it involves the exchange of information, ideas, questions, and concerns. It entails give-and-take. At every practice players are sending us verbal and nonverbal messages. The challenge is to be mindful enough to receive, interpret, and respond in an appropriate and timely manner to needs or uncertainties – be that about instruction on the field or problems off the field. With each of our communication, we convey acceptance and affirmation or rejection and lack of interest. Are we willing to accept those with whom communication is essential, as partners?

Eye contact, facial expression, and tone of voice, body language, all contribute powerfully to a coach's communication. A coach has to be a mindful communicator who is aware of how his words and nonverbal signals are interpreted and understood in the context of his athlete's developmental needs and capacities. The following cases may illustrate the power of communication:

Case 1. A coach recently was heard ripping a little league player for something the player said and a tongue lashing followed. It went something like this, "if you don't like it you can get your stuff and sit up in the stands right now!" When the boy's father was told that his son had said something to the coach, his response was immediate and equally fiery. "Get your stuff now and go to the parking lot. You're done. I mean now". I later asked the player what happened thinking it may be a teachable moment. He shared with me that he was told earlier in the season that he was a team leader and needed to take charge with his teammates in a positive way. So he told the coach that maybe if he didn't yell at them all the time they wouldn't be afraid to make mistakes. The kid expressed confusion as to why he was chastised so strongly and in front of his teammates. So you tell me. Was this mindful communication on the part of the coach? Were his words communicated in the proper context in relation to the developmental level of the player or his capacity to learn from the moment? This is the same kid lauded for his accomplishments as the tourney MVP and the pitcher who just gave them an outstanding performance in the semifinals and helping his team reach the championship game.

Case 2. Many years ago, I was coaching a team of 13-15 year olds. Practice wasn't going well one night. Everyone seemed indifferent and like they wanted to be anywhere else but practice. So for effect, I threw my clipboard against the backstop and said I didn't want us to just go through the motions and if anyone didn't want to be there, they could leave. (Inappropriate then, inappropriate now). We were working on safety and suicide squeeze bunts. One player in particular was inadvertently the focal point of my tirade since he nonchalantly ran home on a squeeze bunt. Fortunately, today he is my friend and I was privileged to coach his sons in high school. He has told me there is no one else he'd rather have than me to coach his kids and that I was the best baseball coach he ever had. Go figure. I learned from that mistake and discovered I didn't know my players; I demonstrated a poor response to the developmental age of the player. I'll never forget the look on his face. He started shaking and crying. It took a while for him to compose himself. I thought the world of this 15 year old kid. It dawned on me this kid overcame a lot to just be there. An alcoholic father and a broken home for starters. The baseball field was his sanctuary. A place where he could escape the turmoil at home and here I was fueling his anxiety and messing with his place of peace.

No doubt each person reading this book has their own communication stories to tell. What might have been a more developmentally appropriate response in the examples above? What message was being sent by the coach in each of these cases? Connecting begins when the other person feels valued. The late University of Texas baseball coach Augie Garrido was always assessing his players, probing their minds, reading their body language, deciphering their wisecracks and comments, and calculating their motivations. He said, "I'm a coach. That's what I do". I can't emphasize enough the relationship building that must be done by coaches in order to be successful. You cannot wait until you need something from players and others. Form a connection. Do something for them along the way so if/when the time comes you need something from them, it is far easier for them to perform the way you would prefer. Do you know the conflicts and fears that your players are carrying? Do you attend other games or events the players in your sport participate in? Do you take an active interest in their lives outside your sport? Do you know their parents, family and friends? Are you authentic in your efforts to know them? What motivates them? What issues are they facing outside your sport? Are you sure to address the *performance* of your players rather than the *performer*?

A recent survey asked coaches and others to share the qualities of the best coach they ever had. What follows is a sample of the responses to the first question:

Patience

Promotes positive environment - did not demean, degrade, embarrass, humiliate

Tolerance for mistakes
Provides precise and positive feedback
Encouraging
Builds confidence
Cares about the development of players
Courageous – makes decisions in the moment that benefit the player, not the scoreboard
Displays passion, engaging, integrity, demanding
Does not "coach" the fun out of the game
Connected to each player
Risk taker
Visionary
Focused
Prepared
Adjusts coaching style to different personalities and learning types
Uses the word NOW – example: Nice catch. **Now** let's work on using two hands.
High energy
Uses Humor
Committed
Trust – made us feel safe to make mistakes
Creative
Demonstrates perseverance when facing adversity
Strives for excellence
Organized
Answers my "Why's"
Taught us to love the effort more than the goal itself
Develops players to fulfill valued roles within the team. Transmits" belief" while developing self esteem
Give parents' roles to make them part of the effort
Vested interest in life outside of sport
Supportive
Really got excited when I did the little things right
Knew every kid's name
Empowering
Gets "buy in"

Now that you have reviewed this list and determined that you possess all these marvelous traits and agree that they are part of your coaching style we can probably stop here, close the book and continue with your present coaching style. You already got it! But wait. Do you really need all these attributes to be successful?

Probably not but the important point here is that the recipient of these coaching traits – the player, parents, and others, thinks they are important. Aren't they our primary stakeholders – the main beneficiary of our work as coaches? That should make it important enough to take note and self-examine our coaching style. A champion-minded coach continually looks for new ways to become better. And yes, sometimes that means not forgetting the good things that got you where you are.

Hot Corner Take Away: People are puzzles of needs wants, drives, and insecurities. Our job as coaches is to find or even be that missing piece for them.

Review the above list. Identify five from the list and think about the ways you either currently exemplify these or how you might demonstrate them in the future.

Preparing Your Game Plan:

1. **Listen Carefully** to:
   - What others expect
   - What others need
   - The correct people
   - Develop trust with others
   - What you say and ensure it has value and purpose
2. **Pay Attention**. In one-on-one and in team meetings focus on what is being said, both verbally and nonverbally. Focused attention helps you zoom into what others are saying giving you a better idea of their moods and feelings.
3. **Recognize the power of non-verbal communication**. Carry yourself in a pleasant, confident, and vigorous manner.
4. **Speak their language**. Champion coaches figure out an athlete's purpose and match it to a process for meeting that purpose. Ask yourself, "What do they care about most? Why does it matter to

them? This shows them you are attuned to their goals and have an understanding of what is important to them. When you speak their language, you scale your message by essentially "talking in color" and painting a vivid picture in their own mind's eye. Get to the "why" behind what you are communicating. This will lead to increased efficiency in performance as you prepare your practices and game plans and help shape new goals based on a mutual understanding of what is important.

5. **Be vulnerable in sharing some information with others**. Coaching is a social process and coaches are the center of it. Be willing to enhance your social skills not just your technical skills with all involved in your program.
6. **Knowledge and communication go hand in hand**. Champion coaches are always learning, and the more you know about something the better you are able to effectively communicate in that area.
7. **Less is more**. Coaches can be guilty of over-communicating in practice and in meetings, giving their audience too many things to work on at once making it hard to accomplish anything. Simplify and try to keep main points to three or less, and see if your players and coaches are better able to focus and achieve the main goals you have set.
8. **Approach communication with grace and truth**. Truth can sometimes create tension and defensiveness in players or others in your program. Grace may lead to people feeling better but without the actual issue being addressed. Creating a blend of truth and grace helps having a more productive conversation.

CHAPTER 2

CHAMPION – HUMILITY

> "I begin with humility, I act with humility, and I end with humility. Humility leads to clarity. Humility leads to an open mind and a forgiving heart. With an open mind and a forgiving heart, I see every person as superior to me in some way; with every person as my teacher, I grow in wisdom. As I grow in wisdom, humility becomes ever more my guide. I begin with humility, I end with humility."

These are Eric Greitens's words to a fellow Navy Seal who struggled mightily with loss, fear, and a search for purpose after returning home from war.

A leader of any sport's program will possess a balance of humility and confidence. Humility allows us to know that we don't have all the answers and that we must continue to get better. Confidence allows us to compete and make decisions as leaders with the trust we are making correct decisions. When George H.W. Bush, our 41st president, was laid to rest, former senator and friend Alan Simpson noted his friend's humility and shared that those who take the high road to humility are not bothered by heavy traffic. True humility is to recognize other's value as well as our own. It is to see there is great opportunity into who others can become, what we can become, and how much more we can do and can be.

The humble coach acknowledges the contributions of others. No great coach or athlete accomplishes anything alone. The humble coach/athlete is gracious in defeat and modest in victory. Sometimes when we lose in sport our opponents were just better, but congratulate them nonetheless. By the way, when we win, no victory dances or celebrations. Realize that victory is a gift.

Every coach loves to coach players who are hungry to win but also humble and yet, how is this done and what kind of effort is put into this? How do we cultivate the virtue of humility? In the age of selfies and Facebook, we are more aware of ourselves than ever before. As we design our social media pages, our LinkedIn profiles to reflect how we want the public to perceive us, humility takes a back seat.

In contrast, humble people don't feel the need to paint a perfect picture of an "ideal life" for others. They have the ability to zoom out and objectively assess the merits or shortcomings of their character. They are committed to the team's success as well as their program. Humble people are more concerned with the quality of their work, the effectiveness of their lives, and the content of their character. True humility is characterized by a quiet confidence and genuine interest in other's realization of their full potential.

Whenever you compare yourself to someone else or decry the fact that you don't have the same education or material things, you set yourself up for disappointment. I call this the scoreboard mentality whereby someone wins and someone loses. Humble people have learned to rid themselves of the cumbersome shackles of comparison. Achieving superiority over others is not a box that humble people are trying to check.

Being released from the burden of comparative score-keeping frees the humble person to concentrate on improving their own performance, character, and moral integrity instead of wasting their energy worrying about how they stack up against others. Humble people do not feel the need to nourish their ego and compare their accomplishments to those of others.

The virtue of humility matters especially for those wishing to *Coach like a Champion*. Humility gives us the freedom to become the leaders we were created to be instead of the person we believe others think we should be. Humility also leads to wisdom. Wisdom helps us become better leaders.

We have an abundance of information at our fingertips daily. How we process that information and turn that into knowledge and make some kind of sense of it is important. The true gift is when we take information and knowledge and form some kind of insight into a learning experience that guides our actions. This is really wisdom.

A person with a *Coaching like a Champion* mindset embraces a humble approach to leadership and understands the whole is greater than its parts. The discipline of humility allows us to rest in the truth that we are part of something much greater than ourselves. It allows us to root for our team, coaches, administrators and all others involved in our program. It inspires those around us, and helps us reach a level of performance that is unattainable without a humble approach. The humble coach asks for input from players, assistants and others and realizes the need for such input and challenges them to bring their unique experiences and expertise to the team/program.

Noted author John Maxwell in, Sometimes You Win—Sometimes You Learn, says the good become the very best due to humility. Humility is foundational to all people who learn from their wins and losses. It is key to success at the highest level. If we become intentional when it comes to promoting the virtue of humility, it is more likely that we will grow in character.

Hot Corner Take Away:

The virtue of humility matters a great deal. It matters not only because it allows us to become better coaches, but because humble coaches are the ones who build the types of teams and programs that are exemplary and make a difference in their communities.

Preparing Your Game Plan:

Sports can be our "school" for the virtue of humility by:

- Giving us a chance to praise and encourage others, rather than seeking the glory for ourselves

- Acknowledging how others made winning possible, and by refusing to let victory puff up our egos
- Realizing that defeat is a part of life so handling it humbly and graciously becomes a part of life
- Understanding and appreciating our limits
- Proving a forum for asking for advice
- Reminding us to praise others
- Being an optimist
- Accepting that we are not the best at everything
- Recognizing our flaws
- Being grateful for what we have – and what we don't

CHAPTER 3

CH**<u>A</u>**MPION – ACCOUNTABILITY

A champion coach is responsible and demonstrates it by taking personal accountability and action for whatever happens. Accountability builds trust not only between players but also the other stakeholders involved in your sport's program. Just as we tell athletes that work and practice are the surest ways to improve, coaches should expect no less of themselves. When things don't go well, they should look at themselves to see where they can make a difference. The coach becomes an active participant in their own cause.

Accountability is developed through a demonstration of daily work habits such as:

- Initiative
- Determination - finishing what you start.
- Submitting yourself to physically demanding work.
- Asking for help if you don't understand.
- Not being so proud that you try to do it alone.
- When you have a list of jobs, doing the toughest ones first. Don't wait to be asked.
- Paying attention to details.
- Making things right when they go wrong.
- Being part of the solution to any problem.

Champion coaches feel and act with a collective spirit and are responsible to their team and other stakeholders. There are four primary fundamentals underlying the *Coaching like a Champion* philosophy:

1. *Coaching like a Champion* will be the most satisfying and enjoyable experience you will ever have.
2. You and every member of your staff/program will experience as much personal and professional growth as possible.
3. You and your staff will form long lasting and meaningful relationships with others.
4. Ensure that you and members of your sport/program remain as competitive as possible, compete for championships and advance as far as you are capable of in the post season.

Coaching like a Champion promotes the concept of "cause over self" and professes that individual achievement will be accomplished through the giving of one's self to the goals and welfare of others. Learn how unselfishness and self-satisfaction can be two of your program's core values.

At sunrise, ask yourself, "How will I be a champion today?". At sunset, you ask, "How was I a champion today?"

Hot Corner Take Away:

All people associated with the sport or program are accountable to each other, not just the coach or the athletic director, etc. They live up to a set of specific standards and attempt to accomplish goals that they helped develop, not the ones imposed on them by authority figures.

Preparing Your Game Plan:

- Ask yourself what type of program do you want to run?
- Who will you involve in the decision making?
- What are your program's core values?
- How do you establish the behavioral expectations associated with these values?

- What consequences have you established if you don't meet these expectations?
- How do you decide the role of your coaches and others in your program?
- What are the desired accomplishments during the season?
- Do you differentiate these into "season goals and progressive benchmarks?
- Do you have an Identity Statement that epitomizes the kind of program and the coach you want to be?

CHAPTER 4

CHA**M**PION – MENTAL TOUGHNESS

> "It isn't hard to be good from time to time in sports. What is tough is being good every day".
>
> Willie Mays, Hall of Fame baseball player.

This quote highlights the importance of consistency and resiliency in sport, despite the competitive situation, or other demands and pressures faced. Mental toughness has consistently emerged in the literature as becoming an increasingly important characteristic of sports in this country. Mental toughness is imperative for peak performance. Let's be honest coaches. We exhort our athletes constantly to hang tough, suck it up, focus, be tough, go pitch by pitch, play by play, etc. We say things like, that kid is really tough; that kid has grit; give me 10 kids like that one. Unfortunately, few of us can clearly define what this means and how our athletes are supposed to apply it. If we cannot define it, how can we train players and others to develop it? I believe it is the ability to remain positive and proactive in the most adverse of circumstances. Mental toughness is built on doing the thing that is hard over and over again, especially when you don't feel like doing it. There are attributes associated with mentally tough performers including:

- Having an unshakable self-belief in the ability to achieve competition goals.
- Having an unshakable self-belief in their unique qualities and abilities that make them better than their opponents.
- Having an insatiable desire and internalized motives to succeed.
- Thriving on the pressure of competition.
- Remaining fully focused in the face of personal life distractions.
- Remaining fully focused on the task at hand in the face of competition-specific distractions.
- Pushing back the boundaries of physical and emotional pain, while still maintaining technique and effort under distress (in training and competition).

Baseball great Cal Ripken identified eight characteristics of perseverance, a term used synonymously with mental toughness, that he felt contributed to his breaking Lou Gehrig's all time consecutive game streak:

- Take the right approach: always be ready to play.
- Have a strong will to succeed: don't let setbacks stop you from achieving your goal.
- Have passion for what you do: love what you do.
- Be competitive: it's not just about beating your opponent. You have to internalize competiveness and take pride in what you do.
- Be consistent: recognize and adjust to change so that you are always able to make a contribution to your team.
- Have conviction: you have to be a little bit stubborn.
- Strength: You have to be in good physical and mental condition. You must be psychological prepared.
- Personal management: don't duck potential problems; take on the problems directly to prevent small problems from building into bigger problems. (Stratton, 2004)

Mental toughness is an important and essential element contributing to performance excellence over time. We all reach critical points in our lives where our mental toughness is tested.

Mental toughness is when a coach can continue to perform their job, to do the job they've been trained to do, regardless of what happens to them in training or competition. For some of us mental toughness may be being able to maintain composure, calm, and control in difficult situations. Whatever the challenge, you have to be strong, see things through a new lens and take decisive action. Sounds easy, doesn't it? After all, we all want to be in a good relationship, be on the same page as our administrators, parents and athletes but it isn't always easy.

It's hard to be mentally tough, especially when you are feeling stuck. Breaking the mold and taking a bold, new direction requires grit, daring, and spunk that only mentally tough people have.

Mentally tough coaches set themselves above the crowd. Where others see impenetrable barrier, they see challenges to overcome.

I saw a story where Thomas Edison had a factory burn to the ground in 1914, destroying a one of a kind prototype and causing $23 million in damage. Edison's response? Thank goodness all our mistakes were burned up. Now we can start fresh again. This is the epitome of mental toughness –seeing opportunity and taking action when things look bleak.

Hot Corner Take Away:

Train athletes and others in your program to continue to perform their job, to do the job they have been trained to do, regardless of what happens to them either in training or competition. Mental toughness can improve confidence, focus, composure and performance.

Preparing Your Game Plan:

Can you build mental strength and toughness? Yes you can. Here's how:

1. **Establish goals**: Consider using the S.M.A.R.T. acronym for goal setting. **S**pecific, **M**easurable, **A**ction-oriented, **R**ealistic, and **T**imely. From a player's perspective but can be adapted to other situations.

- **S**pecific – "I want to improve my footwork when turning the double play" vs. "I want to improve my fielding".
- **M**easurable – "I want to throw more fastballs for strikes" vs. "I want to be a better pitcher".
- **A**ction-oriented – "I will practice my footwork on the double play for an extra 15 minutes every practice" vs. "I will improve my fielding skills".
- **R**ealistic – "I want to limit the other team to 3 runs or less every game that I pitch" vs. "I want to win every game I pitch".
- **T**imely – "I want to throw 5 strikes in a row by the end of the practice session". vs. "I want to throw more strikes".

2. **Motivate Players and Others:**
   Desire – 5 Factors to determine if players really want to be there; to win; to be successful.
   - Drive
   - Determination
   - Leadership
   - Assertiveness
   - Coachability

   Emotional – Factors to determine personal attitudes and feelings about the sport, the coach, and the manner in which they perceive being handled.
   - Confidence
   - Trust
   - Conscientiousness
   - Responsibility
   - Mental Toughness

3. **Mental Imagery**: Vividly see and feel you performing well.
4. **Self-Talk**: Keep thoughts, simple, positive, and powerful.
5. **Confidence**: Have a can do attitude when you need it the most. Perform in the absence of fear, due to the confidence gained in creating situations where players can maximize their talents and pursue their potential to its fullest extent.

6. **Focus**: Stay on target and in the moment.
7. **Mental Toughness**: Do what is hard and stay positive under adversity.
8. **Enjoyment**: Incorporate fun, play, and humor into your game plan and avoid becoming too serious, dull, and uptight.
9. **Body Language**: Carry yourself like a champion. *Warriors don't slouch in battle.*
10. **Positive Affirmations**: Keep in the present moment when creating affirmations. Say" I am" rather than "I will" Some power phrases include:
    - I think, feel, and perform as a champion.
    - I coach with purpose and passion.
    - I have the courage to face and overcome my fears.
    - I will go through fire to pursue my goals and support those in my sport.
    - I am the coach who is most prepared because I do things better than they have ever been done before.
    - I strive to be my best in all conceivable ways.

CHAPTER 5

CHAMPION – PASSION

> "My mission in life is not merely to survive, but to thrive; and to do so with some passion, some compassion, some humor, and some style."
>
> Maya Angelou

I'd like to ask you a few questions. Are you a passionate coach? Do you bring passion every day? Do you keep your high energy throughout the season? Is your passion visible? Are you determined to stay the course, regardless of the circumstances? Do you love to compete? Passion is a strong inclination toward an activity that you like, find important, and invest time and energy. It gets incorporated into who you are. People enjoy activities they are passionate about, and consequently, they invest time and energy in the activities. People who are passionate about an activity value and experience an emotional connection to it. If you are a coach, it is likely you are passionate about athletes, coaching, and sport. It's part of your identity. It gives you pleasure and is a significant part of your identity but does not overpower other aspects of your life. It is truly a gift and is linked to life satisfaction. Passion for your work is a little bit of discovery, followed by a lot of development, and a lifetime of deepening. In my case, my interactions as a youngster with sports deepened my interest and along with the corresponding support and positive feedback received by being a player who could hold his own, propelled my competence, confidence and security. This has no doubt influenced my makeup as a coach. From my early beginnings in the backyard and from the daily games at Curry field on Market street in Somerset, Ohio, my interest and enthusiasm for sport developed and has endured ever since.

Passionate coaches are persistent and will work hard toward their goals. There are two kinds of passion, harmonious and obsessive. Those with obsessive passion are rigid in their persistence and don't experience positive emotions. They continue to persist and push on at sometimes great cost to other aspects of their life. People with harmonious passion on the other hand, are in control of the activity and decide when to engage in it or not. Their persistence is flexible.

Passionate people tend to be successful because they spend a lot of time working on their craft and are continuously learning and trying to improve. They also tend to be flexible in their sport and perform at the top of their game. When you truly love what you are doing it leads to more mastery-oriented goals.

A mastery goal is based on the desire to improve or to beat your previous best. This mastery focus approach also means performing just for the pure joy of it. Renowned college football coach, Nick Saban, said, "It is important that we all make every effort to do what we love. My job is definitely a challenge, but I like what I do so much that it rarely seems like work to me." You think it is a coincidence that Saban has won five national championships in college football?

What every sports program needs are people involved who inspire others with their passion. This makes everyone better. These people constantly renew their commitment to being the best for the team and their program and always come to practice, games, and meetings with energy and passion which becomes contagious. How is this done?

- By fusing passion everywhere possible and helping people believe in themselves.
- Building confidence and self esteem
- Making people feel important and appreciated
- Celebrating and getting excited about others' successes and accomplishments
- Pointing out strengths and contributions of those around you

Coaches will refer to passion as loving an activity, being "all-in" and dedicated to the nth degree, and have specific targets to shoot for in the big picture of life, so much so it can seem uncontrollable at times. For some, it is seen as a form of motivation that is required to do extraordinary things that high performing sports programs require. You may need to be "over-the-top" at times in terms of your outlook on life and your corresponding habits and characteristics. I don't know if that's right or not but passion appears to be a necessary ingredient for *Coaching like a Champion*.

Hot Corner Take Away:

Passion is the soul of significance. It's the fuel. It's the core. For most coaches, passion is formed at an early age from the sheer joy experienced from playing the game. They maintain that joy throughout their life and it appears in the form of vitality, enthusiasm, devotion to their team and relentless pursuit of excellence. You have to have a compelling reason for why you're doing what you do. Every coach should believe that they were put on this earth to fulfill the very purpose of becoming the best version of themselves. Passion can be seen in the daily work of every great competitor. "Champions do not become champions on the court. They are merely recognized on the court. They become champions in their daily routine. Players do not decide their future. They decide their habits, then, their habits decide their future."

Seen on a training room wall.

Preparing Your Game Plan:

- Keep Your Fire Burning. Everyone will feed off your fire. Avoid burning out by regularly relaxing and refreshing your mindset. What changes will you make to bring more passion to your work?
- Take Charge of Your Moods. Recognize your present mental and emotional state and take time to reflect on how your attitudes impact and influence those around you.

- Listen to Those Around You. Spend time with people in your program and attempt to understand their feelings, perspectives, and experiences. Make it a way of life rather than a onetime event.
- Be There for Others. Team building is about recognizing, respecting, and appreciating your teammates. Your friendship can be the encouragement a member of your team might need to make it through a challenging time. The smallest gesture, a simple act of kindness, at just the right time can make a difference.
- Be Genuine. Players, coaches, colleagues, parents, etc., will see right through you if you are phony and superficial. They want you to care about them and help them achieve their goals. Belief in them will breed trust and healthy relationships. Point out others' strengths and contributions – daily.
- Refrain from Excuse-Making. "When your passion and purpose are greater than your fears and excuses, you will find a way." Anonymous.
- Mend Broken Fences. Great coaches are those willing to make mistakes. Durable and enduring relationships are built by pushing through adversity. Conflict is natural. Restore relationships where conflict has caused tension. Be patient, persistent, and pleasant when restoring a relationship.

Adapted from Coaching for Leadership by Cory L. Dobbs, EdD

CHAPTER 6

CHAMPION – INTEGRITY

> "Be more concerned with your character than your reputation. Character is what you really are, reputation is just what people say you are."
>
> John Wooden

Integrity is a simple concept; it is a choice of correct behaviors displayed in small daily decisions. People of integrity engage in actions that follow their words and their beliefs. In other words, their core values and their behavior align. They have a depth of character. This is shown in honesty, sincerity, reliability, respect, humility, and loyalty. It is keeping commitments. It is fulfilling our intentions with actions. It enables us to act out our convictions. Integrity is the foundation of character.

A person of integrity has the ability to pull everything together, to make it all happen no matter how challenging the circumstances. Dr. Henry Cloud explored six qualities of character that define integrity. He shows how people with integrity:

- Are able to connect with others and build trust
- Are oriented toward reality
- Finish well
- Embrace the negative
- Are oriented toward growth

- Have an understanding of the meaning of life

These traits supersede gifts, talents, and ability, and how the ones that have them succeed, and the ones that don't, ultimately fail. The great thing is that all of us can grow in these areas and the journey itself is of great value. Integrity is really the courage to meet the demands that face coaches in e very sport. As coaches we are constantly telling athletes that character counts. We have desired character in ourselves and in the people with whom we work. We have probably felt the effects of integrity when absent, and benefited when it was present. You all know how real it is.

I doubt if there are many among us who do not think they are of reasonable character and demonstrate integrity in our everyday lives. But would you like to improve the way integrity of character really works day to day and how it affects our real results in the areas of life that really matter most. Would you know where to begin in making the personal shift that will make our relationships more fruitful. Are your character traits enabling your talents and abilities to bring you the results that you know you should be getting but somehow are not.

For people of integrity, life is not easier, but it is simpler. A person of integrity will soon face ethical dilemmas, but the choices are simpler because you will apply the same set of personal standards to every dilemma, regardless of how big or small, how public or private.

Remember that inner voice I mentioned in the Introduction? People of integrity have a conscience that remains clear because they listen to the strong inner voices in their life. A coach of integrity says what they mean, their "yes" means yes and their "no" means no, their word is good, their handshake seals the deal and their signature have value. Integrity does not stand by itself; it supports other values such as honor and courage. If you have integrity, nothing else matters and if you don't have integrity, nothing else matters.

What do you stand for as a coach? As a person?

> "One of the ultimate tests of personal character is the willingness and ability to do the right thing despite the costs and risks – to do it without any expectation of

approval or advantage, but simply because it is the right thing to do."

Michael Josephson

I am going to assume that most people reading this book are honest, ethical, and trustworthy. You are faithful to your program and dependable to do the right thing. But ultimately what will make you succeed is who you are as a person. While you may be a person of good character, is something still lacking in your "personhood" that prevents your talents and brains from accomplishing your potential?

Have you wanted more for your program? Have you left the stakeholders in your program wanting more? I think this is a good thing in some respects. Why? Because you and your program are being noticed. Leverage this and you should be able to successfully:

- Gain the complete trust of the people you are leading and capture followers
- See the realities that are in front of you.
- Recognize the blind spots that keep you from reaching your goals.
- Work in a way that produces the outcomes that they should have produced, given their abilities and resources.
- Deal with problem people, negative situations, obstacles, failures, setbacks, and losses.
- Create growth and improvement in your program, people, and the profession.
- Transcend their own interests and give themselves to larger purposes, thus becoming part of a larger mission.

These kinds of issues have little to do with brains, education, training and talent, but instead they have to do with the aspect of character I call makeup and it gets the least amount of attention and work. I have been way too guilty of thinking I can fix everything with increasing my professional skills and knowledge. I read a lot, attend clinics, read blogs, listen to podcasts, watch videos, etc.

Have you ever refused to give up your agenda because of all you had invested in it? You have plenty of integrity and character but you possess a blind spot in failing to recognize the need to regroup because you are "losing' something.

Rarely do we get a course that teaches us about character and relating it to sports. Can you identify the issues of character that relate to your coaching and program? *Coaching like a Champion* requires that you look at a way of thinking about character and its components that if applied, can help you, those who work with you, and your institution, to avoid pitfalls such as:

- Hitting a performance ceiling that is much lower than your aptitude
- Hitting an obstacle or situations that derail you
- Reaching great success only to self-destruct and lose it all

Character = the ability to meet the demands of reality

Do you want people to spend time with you? Then invest time in them. A lesson I learned after many years of experience. As coaches we must get to know the character of each player, coaches, administrator, parent, etc. This takes time but will be well worth it. This is character at work; character with integrity.

If we are to *Coach like a Champion,* we must put our character to work. This will get us to a complete picture of performance, all the way from gaining trust, to getting results, and a return on our hard work and sacrifice. The origins of the word integrity come from the French and Latin meanings of intact, integrate, integral, and entirety. The concept being that the whole thing is working well, undivided, integrated, intact, and uncorrupted. It is really "running on all cylinders". I especially like the definition that encompasses the conditions of being unified, unimpaired, and sound in construction. In short, it is how we are made and this has everything to do with our decision making. Does our handshake mean something? Our signature? No greater compliment can be made than when someone says, "if Steve is involved or thinks it's ok, that's good enough for me". Does this describe you as a coach? If you want to be a champion, it must.

It is not enough to be an aggressive risk taker. You must be able to finish and be a closer. Do not leave good ideas undone, unexecuted, and scattered. None of us is perfect and have all the talent, gifts, and skills we would like. It is not necessary. Dr. Cloud states, however, you do need all the aspects of character while you are putting these gifts to work. You must be able to see the truth of a situation and to see it clearly. Character transcends gifts and the content of the expression of those gifts.

We see extreme examples of this character issue in business, college sports, government, the entertainment industry to name a few. Brilliant people making decisions void of integrity and attention to character. People reading this book probably are not in that category. But are there applications, nonetheless, to our work as coaches or those involved with coaches in some way?

Answer the following:

- Do you exercise the ability to connect authentically?
- Do you have the ability to be oriented toward the truth?
- Do you have the ability to work in a way that gets results and finish well?
- Do you have the ability to embrace, engage, and deal with the negative?
- Are you oriented toward growth?
- Do you have the ability to see the big picture and look beyond yourself or your program?

> "Integrity in its simplest form is purity of intention. It's keeping a clean conscience. But it is also a composite of some of the other mortar qualities in the pyramid. To some extent, integrity contains a bit of reliability, a healthy helping of honesty and a portion of sincerity. However, I believe that the component of purity of intention is important enough to give integrity the status of mortar in its own right."
>
> John Wooden in Pyramid
> of Success book

As coaches we all want our players to be people of integrity. When we have integrity, we are not going to do anything that will be demeaning to anybody else, either on or off the playing arena. To coach like a champion means having and demonstrating the utmost integrity. When I think of people who I think most reflect the quality of integrity it seems the common thread is that they are genuinely concerned about the betterment of others. This sets them apart from others. In the context of *Coaching like a Champion,* this is significant. Wooden asserts that if you are not a sound and honest person, you have no place in the development of our youth. I find it interesting that with all of John Wooden's success, he never had an unlisted phone number. He always made an effort to visit anyone who sought his help. People from all walks of life received encouragement from him whether it was a phone call, visit, or a letter.

Hot Corner Takeaway: So how do you demonstrate integrity in your interaction with players and others? How is integrity reflected in your philosophy of coaching? Are you intentional in the way you demonstrate respect and kindness for others?

Preparing your Game Plan:

1. Fulfill your promises. To your players, staff, stakeholders. Deliver on promises.
2. Keep appointments. This affects you professional and personally. Be present for those who count on you. Listen, engage, and follow through.
3. Before you make a commitment, stop and reflect on whether you can deliver. It may be best to "under promise and over deliver," as the adage goes.
4. Get comfortable with saying no. No one can say yes to everything and follow through on it all.
5. Examine how you react in knee-jerk situations as well as how you make longer term commitments (e.g., attending events, completing projects, etc.) Use this introspection to become self-aware, keep score and improve.
6. Polish your communication skills. Fuzzy communication can lead to unfulfilled promises. Proofread all communications before you distribute them.

7. Consider the habits and skills you need to develop to enhance your integrity. Stop behaviors such as sugar coating or speaking impulsively. Take great care with the language you use especially in dealing with sensitive issues like racism, sexual preference, and religion. We are living in an emotionally charged climate where our words are measured often and social media expedites reactions from others to your words. Improving your personal courage will cause others to take note and allow you to contain any potential damage from words spoken.
8. Avoid people who lack integrity. Your character will be judged by the character of your friends and acquaintances.

Gauging your Integrity:

- Am I willing to say what I am thinking?
- Am I willing to risk being wrong?
- Does this conduct make me a better person?
- Am I leading by example?
- Am I taking 100% responsibility?

CHAPTER 7

CHAMPIO̲N – OVERCOMING ADVERSITY

> "Of all the virtues we can learn, no trait is more useful, more essential for survival, and more likely to improve the quality of life than the ability to transform adversity into an enjoyable challenge."
>
> Mihaly Csikszentmihalyi

How many times in the past week have you felt that the stress associated with coaching, playing, or being part of a sport's program is becoming way too stressful? "Is this all there is to life?" Do you ever think that something is missing? If you find yourself burning the candle at both ends or feeling like you are juggling too many responsibilities, you may need more resilience – the ability to persevere and adapt when things go awry. Everyone needs resilience because one thing is for certain, life includes adversities. More paperwork, new state regulations, parent demands, personnel issues, etc. Some of these may be major issues such as a failed relationship, family illness, and financial problems. A lack of resilience affects your level of success at work and in life. How resilient are you? Can you face your challenges bravely and confidently or do you feel like giving up?

The reality is that you are probably pretty good at dealing with obstacles but none of us are perfect nor do we have all the abilities that we need to combat adversity fully. How do we do this and what do we need? No doubt you have the dedication and determination to do well or you probably would not be reading this book. *Coaching like a Champion* requires more than just determination and commitment. The hallmark of a true champion is *tenacity*. In this context, we are talking about achieving results over a long period of time, not just once in a while. We are talking about an *informed* tenacity and the resolve to make things better for the program in specific ways and in spite of inconveniences, obstacles, or the effort required. The champion will exert endless determination and conviction that leads to breakthroughs and real progress. Champions have a burning fire inside of them, and find satisfaction in the journey because of the lofty goals they have set and their belief and dedication to the process to get there. They have no interest in settling for usual outcomes, and they push beyond basic expectations. They have an unstoppable will to move forward, build momentum, and to create a following of supporters along the way. *Coaching like a Champion* requires the ability to adapt and bounce back when things don't go as planned. Resilient people don't wallow or dwell on one failure. They acknowledge the situation, learn from their mistakes, and move forward. Resilient people consciously control meaning through their focus. In other words, if you choose to focus on how great your life is, the more you will notice the great things in your life. If you focus on the opportunities provided by your sport and your involvement with it, you will begin to see opportunities you would have missed before. On the other hand, if you focus on what you are lacking in life, you will begin to notice a lot more areas of your life where you are lacking.

Champions are tireless, have stamina, and devise tactics to not only keep things going but execute new ideas and implement game-changing initiatives. Make no mistake; this can be stressful to always being in motion and on the upswing constantly. But champions know how to make progress and in spite of demands and fixing things on the fly and looking for a better tomorrow. At times, pressing through and overcoming the inevitable disruptions, resistance, and obstacles takes tremendous effort. Let's face it coaches: just keeping up with the day-to-day routine and all the problems associated with it can be exhausting. Here's the rub: When daily demands are compounded with the need to invest energy, time, and resources in an attempt to be on top all the time, it can feel a bit grueling.

But your followers will see your fierce commitment to the process and your relentless resolve and determination to finish what you believe in.

Conversely, some of us have no doubt been involved with leaders who have gone to the extreme with tenacity. They have trouble letting go of bad ideas, and it can become of battle of wills, competing ideas, and people are left wondering about the direction they are going or being led. This creates an environment of defensiveness and fear and stifles forward progress.

Think of your life as a kind of lens through which you view your life and all of the challenges that it brings. But sometimes it is life's inevitable misfortunes that can actually serve as a fuel to propel us into even better place. Resilience is the ability to shut down – but you fight on. Resilient people have both tapped and untapped reserves, enabling them to overcome and thrive as they face the setbacks, challenges, and fears of daily life. Sometimes our problems can become our greatest resources. So coaches who are currently or aspiring to *Coaching like a Champion* must be relentless if you wish to forge ahead despite the problems confronting you.

Hot Corner Take Away

The ability to persevere and overcome is a key in helping champions achieve their goals.

Overcoming adversity is the capacity of to prepare for disruptions and recover, adapt, and grow from the disruptive experience. You also develop greater capacity to bounce back from a crisis, learn from it, and achieve revitalization. As coaches become more adept at managing disruptions and the unforeseen, they become better at creating and taking advantage of new opportunities in good times and bad. Champions cannot merely return to normal functioning after a disruption, they can achieve significant transformation.

Preparing Game Plan

5 action steps to build your resiliency:

1. **Positive Mindset**: See abundance in the world and recognize change as an opportunity, not a threat.

2. **Awareness**: If change causes you stress, stop ruminating on it. Take control of your life and do not blame others, or outside circumstances. The more responsibility you accept, the more empowered you become.
3. **Adaptability**: embrace uncertainty, take risks, and learn to go with the flow. The more mindful and present you become, the more open you will be.
4. **Perseverance**: Create an arsenal of good habits that you can implement to endure any situation and overcome any obstacle.
5. **Resourcefulness**: You don't have all the answers and refusing to ask for directions will only get you more lost. You are not in this alone. Seek out people, groups or resources and ask for help.
6. The more you practice resilience, the faster you will be able to recover from the inevitable setbacks you will encounter.

CHAPTER 8

CHAMPION**N** – NEVER SETTLE

"Champions do not become champions when they win an event, but in the hours, weeks, months, and years they spend preparing for it. The victorious performance itself is merely a demonstration of their championship character."

Michael Jordan.

From the first time I threw a baseball in my backyard with my dad I was hooked on sports. When I saw the glean in his eye when I zipped the ball back to his glove with some snap to it, I knew we had something to which we could bond. He was demanding in what he expected of us kids and held us accountable for the chores assigned to each of us. But for a brief time the hardness of his demands subsided when we were in that backyard. I kept getting better and better and I will never forget the smile on his face when I bested my best friend in a pitcher's duel as a 12 year old on opening day. My buddy Jack threw a no-hitter and I allowed a single hit but managed to win on an unearned run. To my dad it may have well been the World Series. That very summer my dad was injured in a gas well explosion that left him with an aneurism requiring brain surgery. He was never the same. It would be a few years before we could even play catch again but by this time he was a different personality. We had little in common and I lost the dad I knew. But through it all we shared a common love of the game of baseball and even though he had memory problems, he never forgot the one hit gem that beat the Tigers on opening day. I believe this experience profoundly affected my love of the game and sense of competition. I always wanted to please my dad and thus worked extremely hard for that recognition. I found myself pouring myself into sports, school work, and everything other endeavor. I wanted to be good because that's where I got my praise and recognition. From the countless trips to Curry Field, a local sandlot, to the outdoor basketball court at my school, I was somebody. My work ethic started at these places and from those early experiences, I was wired to never settle for anything but my best. I wanted approval from everyone and it became a big part of who I was. This worked well in my youth but more substance would be required of me as I progressed through life.

Fast forward to age 21 where I found myself married to my high school sweetheart and a senior in college. I finished my undergraduate degree in Education and got a job in the local school district. Not bad considering I was a first generation college student and eventually would earn a Master's and Doctorate in education. I say this not to brag but to illustrate that I always believed no one would outwork me. I may not be the sharpest knife in the drawer at times but I can work harder than anybody else. I approach everything that way including coaching. Incidentally, I was hired as an assistant varsity football coach and an assistant varsity baseball coach. I worked tirelessly to get up to snuff with football after only having a couple of years' experience as a football player on a small high school squad. After two years I discovered it was not for me but I enjoyed the baseball experience immensely and became the head coach after two years. I was offered to start an American Legion summer program and that fueled a love affair with the game.

I tell you this because I firmly believe it set the tone for my present work ethic and how I approach each and every endeavor in my life. I am highly organized and having other's respect is vital to me. I have learned later that forming relationships and engaging all those as part of my program is essential, vital, and immeasurable. It takes time, commitment, and energy along with an overall wherewithal to be successful.

To be a true competitor requires possessing a champion's heart. They have a visible courage that others want to emulate. It does not disappear or waiver in times of difficulty, but rather it steps up in times of crisis. People of courage get emotional in a quiet way, but their character is obvious to everyone.

Their strength is developed through determination, ambition, motivation, commitment, perseverance and personal character. Champions become stronger and more resilient because they make promises to themselves and then keep them. People will follow what you do before they follow what you say.

Having courage doesn't mean you are going to avoid tough times, but the competitor has a heart of a lion. Their heart doesn't understand the concept of "quit". When you combine their strong heart and their talent they become a warrior. Champions are not intimidated by pressure, they thrive on it.

All the ideas presented here are essential but none can tie them all together like the following:

> *"To every man there comes that special moment in his lifetime, when he is figuratively tapped on the shoulder and offered the chance to do a very special thing, unique to him and fitted to his talent; what a tragedy if that moment finds him unprepared or unqualified for the work which should be his finest hour."* Winston Churchill

How easy is it for you to do the following? Your answers will say volumes about how you build momentum toward a *Never Settle* mentality:

- **Take risks**. Doing something out of the ordinary each day. Leveraging what you have today for what you have tomorrow.
- **Get outside you zone of comfort**. Learn new skills. Would you consider technology, data, and analytics?
- **Never stop learning**. Increase your value. Apply your new found knowledge and experiment with it at every step of your journey to the top.
- **Speak to yourself every day**. Don't worry about what others say about you. It is what you say about you that matters. Others are not in your way. You may be in your way. Great spirits encounter violent opposition from mediocre minds.

- **Surround yourself with the best people.** Be diverse thus adding creativity, problem solving, and productivity to the team.
- **Work hard.** Work consistently. Work to adapt. Never think you have to do anything. You must want to do it. Cultivate discipline and have the heart to invest time in things that are meaningful to you. Do not act on the momentum of other people's expectations. Cultivate an attitude of certainty and follow through on your words. The difference between mediocrity and excellence is often a matter of effort. Some of us throw our gifts away on a life of mediocrity.

  Great people throw everything they have into their gifts and achieve a life of success, which transcends with the progression of their craft.

  It is much easier to accept things as they are, to go with the flow but there is danger in in that. When we fail to challenge the status quo (the way things are), we fail to bring much needed change in our lives. If we want our lives to make a difference we have to be willing to be uncomfortable and to make others uncomfortable in the process. You cannot make meaningful change without shaking things up.

- **Never stop evolving** in terms of efficiency, effectiveness, and evaluation.

Hot Corner Take Away: *Never Settle* epitomizes the spirit and relentless pursuit of excellence. Stephen Covey, author of The Seven Habits of Highly Successful People said, "The main thing is to keep the main thing the main thing." *Coaching like a Champion* requires focusing on the main thing amidst the massive amount of distractions that is guaranteed to come your way. Eliminate clutter that keeps you from accomplishing the task at hand. There are no shortcuts to excellence. Developing real expertise, figuring out really hard problems, it all takes time – longer than most people imagine.

Preparing Your Game Plan:

Every day, every practice, and every moment in your life should be leading you towards something special. Your effort and attitude everyday will determine what that something is. Champions are motivated to work towards something each and every day for years and years.

- Don't waste opportunities. Don't waste a day.
- Improve yourself each and every day.
- Make it a daily goal to get better and better.
- Focus on fundamentals.
- Learn something constructive from every defeat.
- LOSS - Learning Opportunity Stay Strong– within every loss – of any kind – there is a crucial lesson you're supposed to learn.
- Time catches up with all of us and if you don't pursue your dreams now, your "someday" may never come.
- The only thing that can stop you is you. Don't complain, don't blame, and don't ever quit on your dream.
- Never give up. F.A.I.L. means, "First Attempt in Learning".
- E.N.D. means, "Effort Never Dies".
- "No" as an answer, remember N.O. means, "Next Opportunity".

EPILOGUE

I just penned my first book. A pretty big accomplishment from this small town boy from humble beginnings. I have already discussed some of the reasons for writing *Coaching Like a Champion* but this Epilogue is challenging because I want to wrap up the book in stupendous fashion and this is difficult for this very ordinary guy. But here goes.

I believe what I am today was formed early on the playgrounds, ball fields, and gymnasiums in a small Midwest town in Ohio. It could have been Anywhere USA and like thousands of other youth back in the day we made our own fun every single day. No techie stuff to play with. Any activity that involved a ball was the primary interest. I learned a curve ball from Gary C. and how to hit by waiting for ping pong balls to come off the roof of Bobby D's roof. Intense games involving whiffle ball were organized by Barney at "Pompey stadium". I'm convinced that I learned how to hit off the best whiffle ball pitchers my hometown had to offer. No video-taped at bats, no You Tube hitting drills, no clinics; just regular and consistent games for the sheer joy of it. Bobby D and I would spend hours at the little league field throwing up rubber balls and honing our fielding skills and improving our hand-eye coordination. If it wasn't baseball, J.D. and I were on the basketball court playing intense pick-up games with older high school kids who demanded a lot of us. I thought I was a pretty good scorer but Andy K would remind me constantly how important it was to play defense. A fact that must have been lost on me because I have the distinction of allowing one of our high school foes to break his high school's single game scoring record with me guarding him. It gets worse. He broke it again the next game we played each other.

So what, right? What's the big deal? Let me explain. I *connected* with all those people mentioned above. They were my world, my escape when things were maybe not so great at home. Don't get me wrong. I had parents who loved me and all my basic needs were met but there were difficult moments with my dad's injury, losing siblings at a young age, and my mom struggling while working 2-3 jobs. No sob story intended here. But in my escape to sports, all was A-Okay. I learned street smarts. I could mask my inner turmoil by pretending to be one of my high school or professional heroes on the basketball court. Barney and I would pretend to be the feared M & M boys (Mickey Mantle, Roger Maris) as part of our batting order for out Little League All Star team. I had an instant identity and a bond with these "heroes". Couple that with the fact I peddled newspapers all around town at 4:30 a.m. every day for years. On Saturday's I would go to each customer and collect for the week. I learned that to say, "Yes sir, yes ma'am and thank you would earn you adult respect no matter what side of the tracks you think you were born on. It also taught me that dedication, goal setting, determination and effort were appreciated, rewarded, and recognized.

So let's fast forward to today. All my childhood contacts shaped me in some fashion. I learned to never quit, jump back up when knocked down and *connect* with as many people as possible who could help me in my life. I didn't realize at the time I was formulating and molding my values for the future. I suspect we all do this but it reinforces the fact that others in our life have tremendous influence and transformative potential on our lives and can help in shaping our future interactions and goals. Hear me coaches? Teachers? Never underestimate the power of your words and of your example.

When my two kids were born, I was a changed man. I could not wait to hold them and be with them every day. At the time, I did not know that coaching would be part of my life. I never set out to be a coach. I wanted to be the best person I could be and as life evolved it became important to me that I strive to be the best in all of my life's roles – husband, son, dad, teacher, coach, uncle, etc. As one gets older and becomes more firmly grounded in life and his faith in a Higher Power, it all starts coming together. Everyone wants to "arrive" so to speak. I mean isn't it nice that we have people come up to us at some point, maybe years later, and say something like, "this is my coach from high school. He was the best fundamental guy I was ever around". This actually happened to me one time as I was attending a funeral and I had not seen the deceased's son for almost 30 years. In fact, this former player was one that I least expected to say favorable things about me since I remember him not being thrilled about the amount of playing time he was receiving. In fact, he brings his high school son over to me and makes a big deal about my being his coach in high school. What he remembered was the importance of practicing like we never won a game and then playing the game like we never lost. He went on to say that he used this same approach in coaching his kids in youth sports.

I went to a wedding of one of my summer college kids and the family insisted I sit in the front row with them because I was "family". I attended another wedding of a former player and he confides in me that he just found out that day he was cut by the New York Yankees organization. What a bitter sweet day. He marries the love of his life but gets divorced from one of the strongest franchises in all of baseball and sees his boyhood dream start to fade. We embraced and discussed how this might become an opportunity for something better. I will never forget him saying that God had a plan for him and he was going to place his trust in God to show him the way. The teacher became the student that day and I have always admired how this former player rebounded from this setback with such strength. By the way, he chose to not get back into baseball by trying out for another team. Instead he chose a path of ministry and remains active in that capacity to this day.

I started coaching in an era where it seemed ok to be tough and demanding; where it was my way or the highway. I can honestly share with you that I can clearly differentiate that period in my life from the more recent period whereby I consciously tried to make *connecting* with the players more of a priority. This is when I took more interest in them as individuals and made it a point to embrace them in a baseball fraternity or family. No matter the player's status on the team, if they were on that team, they were forever a member of the family. This has been rewarding and I wish I could have those early years back. I would be checking my ego at the door, emphasizing fairness over consistency, valuing the person over the player, *connecting* before directing, and always looking for the teachable moments.

But perhaps the best testimony of influence is with my own kids. My son was fortunate enough to play college baseball and my wife Peggy and I followed him through all four years including spring trips to Florida and league road trips to Tennessee, Texas, Kentucky, and Georgia, and Indiana. These trips commenced from our home in southeastern Ohio. In an exit interview for the college newspaper our son commented that, "Before each game I survey the stands and look for my parents. When I see them, I know all is good and I am ready to play the game". It still makes me a little weepy eyed to read that. During his high school Hall of Fame induction, he reiterated his appreciation for our constant support and the sacrifices we made so he could play the game he truly loves. Of course the pleasure was all ours.

I found a book he gave me for Father's Day in 1996, a year before he graduated from high school. It was an illustrated history of baseball and he wrote on the inside cover:

Dad,

*"I wanted to give you a signed home run ball for Father's Day but that ended up being about 10 feet short, so I guess this book will have to do. Thanks for always working with me and helping me get better. It really means a lot". **Zach***

Even his home games were out-of-state so it was tough at times after working all day and traveling to get to the ball park in time. But ask anyone who ever did it and they will all say they would not change a thing. The moral of the story is that players and kids will remember the effort you made to be part of their lives and support them.

My daughter is special as well. Although she didn't have much interest in athletic participation, she enjoyed watching sports and was a member of her high school cheerleading squad. I am most proud that she was one of her brother's biggest supporters and would also travel long distances to watch him play. One of my more prized possessions is the inscriptions she makes in books she buys for me. They are always touching and heartfelt while hitting on some point she finds admirable. You never can get enough of these.

Here's an example:

Dear Dad –

Many of my fondest memories involve my love of "America's Favorite pastime". Thanks for your time and effort in helping Zachary and I appreciate all of life's simple pleasures! You can take me out to the ballpark any day! I love you!
Amanda

Although this book is written primarily for those involved in coaching athletes, it has applications to anyone involved in some capacity with any sports program. The message meant to be conveyed is that coaches need to pay close attention to the messages they are sending to all involved in their programs. So much has been written about our expectations for athletes and less about how coaches' are supposed to go about this business with the key stakeholders involved in their sport's program. It is my sincere hope that you enjoy the journey to *Coaching Like a Champion* and embrace the 8 essential building blocks outlined in the book to fully realize the tremendous potential for being significant as well as a difference maker with all those with whom you have contact not only in sports but in life.

What you do really matters. I hope you believe that!

REFERENCES AND RECOMMENDED READING

Afremow, Jim, PhD., *The Champion's Mind*: *How Great Athletes Think, Train, and Thrive* New York, NY: Rodale, 2013

Bartholomew, Brett. *Conscious Coaching: The Art & Science of Building Buy*-In Omaha, Nebraska: Bartholomew, Strength LLC

Brubaker, John. *Seeds of Success: Leadership, Legacy, and Life Lessons* Learned New York, NY: Morgan James Publishing, 2016

Cain, Brian. *The 12 Pillars of Peak Performance: A Story About Becoming a Peak Performer Peak* Performance Publishing, 2016

Carroll, Pete, Roth, Yogi, and Garin, Kristoffer, A. *Win Forever: Live, Work, and Play Like a Champion* New York, NY: Penguin, 2011

Csikszentmihalyi, Mihaly. brainyquote.com

Churchill, Winston.azquotes.com

Covey, R. Stephen. *The 7 Habits of Highly Effective People* New York, NY: Simon & Shuster: 1989

Cloud, Henry, Dr. *Integrity*: *the Courage to Meet the Demands of Reality* New York: NY Harper Collins, 2006

Creasy, John, Wayne, Jr. *An Analysis of the Components of Mental Toughness in Sport, Dissertation*, Virginia Polytechnic Institute & State University, 2005

Dare to be a Champion Newsletter, 2018 www.daretobechampions.com

Daugherty, Travis. *The Lens: Raising A Champion Athlete & Man in Today's Myopic World*, coachtravisdaugherty@gmail.com 2017

Dobbs, Cory. *Coaching for Leadership*, sports leadership.com 2018

Duckworth, Angela. *GRIT: The Power of Passion and Perseverance* New York, NY: Scribner, 2016

Ehrmann, Joe. *InSideOut Coaching: How Sports can Transform Lives* New York, NY: Simon & Shuster, 2011

Garrido, Augie, Smith, Wes. *Life is Yours to Win: Lessons Forged from the Purpose, Passion, and Magic of Baseball* New York, New York: Touchstone, 2011

Goldsmith, Marshall. *Demonstrating Integrity: A Key Characteristic of the Future Global Leader* wabccoaches.com

Goldsmith, Wayne. *Mental Toughness: What is It and How to Coach It* Business Coaching Worldwide June 2008 Vol 4, Issue 2 wgcoaching.com

Gordon, Jon, Smith, Mike. *You Win In the Locker Room First: The 7 C's to Build a Winning Team in Business, Sports and Life* Hoboken, New Jersey: Wiley & Sons, Inc., 2015

Greitens, Eric. *Resilience.* New York, NY: Mariners Books, 2015

Grover, Tim, S. *Relentless: From Good to Great to Unstoppable* New York, NY: Scribner, 2013

Josephson, Michael. azquotes.com

Maxwell, John, C. *Everyone Communicates. Few Connect* Harper Collins Leadership, 2010

Maxwell, John, C. *Intentional Living: Choosing a Life That Matters* Center Street Publishing, New York, NY: 2015

Maxwell, John C. *Sometimes You Win, Sometimes You Learn* New York, NY: Center Street Publishing, 2015

Mays, Willie. quotefancy.com

McCaw, Allistair. *7 Keys to Being a Great Coach: Become Your Best and they Will Too* Allistair McCaw: 2016

Saban, Nick. *How Good Do You Want To Be? A Champion's Tips on How to Lead and Succeed* New York, Ballantine Books, 2005

Stewart, Chris M. *Building Champions.* Chris Stewart, Athens, Ohio, 2018

Stottlemyre, Todd. *9 Point System for Major League Achievement: Relentless Success, Don't Quit* Issaqua, WA: Made for Success Publishing, 2017

Stowell, Steven, J. Ph.D., Mead, Stephanie, S., MBA. *The Art of Strategic Leadership: How Leaders at All Levels Prepare Themselves, Their Teams, and Organizations for the Future* Hoboken, New Jersey: John Wiley & Sons Inc., 2016

Stratton, R. (2004). *Ripken on Perseverance: Coaching Youth Sports* quoted in Creasey, John, Wayne, Jr. *An Analysis of the Components of Mental Toughness* in Sport, Dissertation, Virginia Polytechnic Institute & State University, 2005

Tressel, Jim, Fabry, Chris. *The Winners Manual for the Game of Life* Carol Stream, Illinois: Tyndale House Publishers, 2008

Truelove, Amanda, A. *Mental Toughness Training Intervention for Collegiate Track and Field Athletes* Master's Thesis, University of Western Ontario, 2014

Tutko, Thomas, H. *Toughness Learning Curve* media. hometeamsonline. com 1985

Vallerand, Robert, J. *The Psychology of Passion: A Dualistic Model* Oxford University Press, Oxford, England, U.K., 2015

Welch, John, C. *Mastering the Power of GRIT: Strategies, Tactics, and Tools from the Heroes of* Tenacity, *Resilience, and Guts* San Diego, CA: By the People Books, 2016

Wooden, John, Carty, Jay. *Coach Wooden's Pyramid of Success Ada, Michigan:* Baker Publishing Group, 2009

CPSIA information can be obtained
at www.ICGtesting.com
Printed in the USA
BVHW031323210621
610133BV00013B/79

9 781984 572899